Walking in Beauty

HARRY K. ROBERTS

2011

Photographs courtesy of Trinidad Museum Society and Humboldt State University Library, Roberts Photograph Collection.

Front Cover: Sunrise In The High Country
Back: Harry Roberts In 1977. Photos By Esther Roberts

ISBN: 0-966-4165-4-6

The Press at Trinidad Art

Trinidad, California

© 2011

Contents

Foreword

Harry K. Roberts' fundamental teaching was, 'be true to yourself.' In this he followed an important tenet of Yurok Indian ethics. One's real self and its purpose in life (they are one and the same) is a manifestation of the indescribable, what Harry called "Creation," pure "Beauty"; reality as it actually is. It is a human being's particular opportunity and responsibility to discover his or her real self and purpose and through it, Creation. This book of stories, poems, short essays and commentaries is Harry's account of his own discovery, during his childhood and early manhood, of himself and his purpose in life.

Harry was born in about 1906 in an Irish-American family living in San Francisco's East Bay. His father was an accountant for a canning company and, beginning when Harry was 11, the family spent summers--from the spring to the fall runs of salmon--in the Yurok village of Requa, at the mouth of the Klamath River on the Pacific coast near California's Oregon border. His father, Harry C. Roberts, was in management at a large salmon cannery that employed, almost exclusively, Yurok and other California Indian fishermen and cannery workers. Robert (Frank) Spott, the adoptive son of the headman of Requa, Captain Spott, was the factory's liaison in Requa and the Spotts and the Roberts became close friends. Harry played with the children of the Spott household and, in time, Robert Spott, a highly regarded spiritual and political leader, became Harry's medicine teacher; his Uncle.

Harry was taught by Robert Spott from childhood until his early thirties. Through Robert and other Yurok elders, Harry was trained in a traditional Yurok way, first as a "real man" (an independent person who others can depend on) and then as a "high man" with medicine for "philosophy," as people say today --in Harry's case, a counselor and teacher. In the 1970s, after active and widely varied experience in the world, he attracted many, primarily non-Indian students. He taught them what they individually asked to learn, whether farm management, wild plant identification, craft skills, or spiritual practice. He died near San Francisco Zen Center's Green Gulch Farm, in Marin County, California, in the spring of 1981. Green Gulch's large practice hall was filled to overflowing for his funeral.

In 1976 Harry had begun to pull together many stories and poems and notes on training topics that he had written over the years. Together with the anthropologist Thomas Buckley, who edited the material and transcribed Harry's oral commentaries on the poems and stories, he completed the first draft of a short book in 1978. In the next two years Harry went over the draft with Yvonne Rand, changing little in the text but rearranging the order of stories and poems, finishing the reordered draft in 1980. A copy of the manuscript was given to the late Ned Simmons of Trinidad, California, but copyright disputes delayed its publication.

Although two stories and two poems appeared in magazines during Harry's lifetime, the book manuscript languished for many years, due to no fault of Ned's. This was a shame: Harry never intended to make a fuss over his *Walking in Beauty* but wanted to see it in print as a modest account of growing up Yurok, a small book of "little stories," a gift to those who might be able to see Beauty in it. (He explains the poems that are included with the stories in his own Introduction.) Harry's original idea was to publish his book in the format of an old-time McGuffey's Reader for school children. *Walking in Beauty* is that and far more.

Harry Roberts was a complex man, neither Irish nor Yurok, a lot of both, representing himself as neither. Utterly pragmatic, Harry was also a yarn-spinner and a romantic and in telling stories from a Native perspective he risks appearing as yet another Earnest Thompson Seton, a co-founder of the Boy Scouts of America. To take him as such would be a mistake. His knowledge ran very deep and was entirely authentic, founded in his earned experience.

Walking in Beauty may be read on many levels but on each Harry's profound understanding, deep intention and wisdom, his pure enjoyment of all life and of Beauty itself, shine through clear and bright. It is a book that deserves many re-readings and careful consideration and it is good that it is finally available to a general readership, as Harry all along intended it to be.

--Jōkan Zenshin
Ogawadera
Fall 2011

Harry Roberts in 1911

Introduction

HARRY ROBERTS

These are stories about a child growing up in a predominantly Yurok Indian community, about 1915. Though the material is primarily factual, the stories are in no way anthropological but are intended to give the reader some flavor of Indian life as a growing child experienced it. For example, in former times the Brush Dance was given for adults and children. At present [1978] it is only for children.

The short poems are intense, compressed statements, often used as teaching devices in the Yurok medicine tradition. They are designed to provoke responses: questioning one's experience, puzzling over life's ambiguities, surfacing deep feelings. In this way they share common purpose with many esoteric teaching traditions throughout the world. In addition to being used for teaching, they were often used in formal address to council meetings. If, for example, a speaker wanted to emphasize the point that what you see depends on how you look at it, he would quote the poem on sea foam [p. 60]. After all, is sea foam ocean or is it air?

The Rock

In the beginning there was a rock. It was quite a large rock and it was made of everything that was. Very gradually this rock took shape and moved around and made itself ready for that which was to be.

It felt empty and barren, and lonesome and unloved. And so it cried. There was nowhere for the tears to go except upon the face of the rock, so that is where they stayed, running down the creases, making rivers. The rivers flowed together and made the ocean. The ocean made clouds and sent back clean water over the rock to wash its face. The rivers piled up the cleanings and made soil. It was then that the rock was no longer just a rock, but had made itself ready to become an earth.

So, the first living parts of creation were the sun and the stars and the earth.

The Dog

I was sitting by the spring just gazing across the river and wondering. Small boys often do--they don't really know what they wonder about. So, I was wondering. My dog was sitting beside me, looking at me as though he was just wondering, too.

Uncle came quietly up the trail and found us so. He stood looking at us for a while and finally asked what we were wondering about. I told him that I was just wondering, and wondered why my dog seemed to be wondering too. Uncle said that this was just naturally so, and then he told me this story:

"In the beginning when the Wo-gay were here it became the days when it was time for them to go and let the Indians be here.[1] The Creator gave them a choice of what they wanted to do. One wanted to become the redwood tree so that he could furnish people with houses and boats. Others wanted to be other things, and still others wanted to go back to the spirit lands. One man, who was especially good, was chosen by the Creator to be the father of the human beings.

"So it came about that this man and his female dog lived on top of a hill, and when the flood came to wash the world clean he and his dog were left above the waters.

"After the flood, the man and his dog became man and wife, and after a while she gave birth to a girl-child. But it was so hard for the dog to have a half-human child that she died. The man raised the child and when she grew up he married her. She, too, gave birth to a girl but, because she was half dog, she couldn't survive the birth of this human-like child and she died. Again the man raised a daughter and again he married her. But this time they had a boy-child, and then a girl-child. These children were the first human beings, and when they grew up they married. All of us come from them."

Uncle said, "So you see, you are part dog and that is why the dog is the only animal that can understand people. That is also why you cannot kill a dog--because it would be murder."

One who does not make his own trail can never approach Creation

This is Robert Spott's. It came up sometime during the course of study, as such things do. The study goes slowly, a little here, a little there. Hard study may go on for six years or so. You go off, do this and that, come back. In the course of time things naturally come along.

This is so obvious that it needs little comment. You cannot approach Creation through other people's thoughts or through their ways. You have to make your own path: you clear the brush out, shove the rocks out of the way. But then, no one else can use it to advantage. If you let them try, they'll blame you if they don't make it. You can't use another's path because you don't know what stones have been taken out or what was done with them. Through ignorance you will trip over them or put them back in the path. You will not learn anything because it was already done for you. Or so you thought.

Coot

It was nearing sunset and the afternoon was cast with long shadows. Hi-pur and I were frantically weaving tule floats, hoping to get them done before it got too dark, for the coots had come to settle on the lagoon and the waters were black with them.

Tule floats were made to look like a mass of floating tules, only they were shaped like a doughnut so that you could put your head through the hole and be masked from the ducks or coots or other water birds. You took a small log that would just keep you afloat and you straddled it as though riding a horse, putting your head up through the tule float. Then you slowly drifted and paddled your way into the mass of birds, grabbed their feet under water, and pulled them down. Under water, you wrung their necks and put them in a sack that hung from your belt. This was the best way to get coots or ducks as the birds in the flock never got nervous or disturbed and so didn't fly off.

We got our floats built in time and went after the coots and caught several of them. But this was our first experience in "fishing" for birds this way and it seemed so easy that I got over-confident. I miss-grabbed one and it got away, flying off screaming like a banshee, whereupon all of the rest of the flock took off.

When I told Uncle what had happened he laughed and said, "That is why the old men never answer questions on the day they are asked. Don't get over-hasty. Each bird is a new experience, and each has a first time to be caught. So does each idea."

Robert Spott ca. 1920

Brush Dance Wand

Uncle was sitting in the morning sun in front of his house fixing the feathers on the long head wands for the Brush Dance. He had made a pot of sturgeon glue and was very carefully smoothing the feathers down and gluing new feathers in where the old ones were damaged or torn loose. He was working very carefully and slowly for this was very fine, difficult work to do.

I looked over one of the wands that he was repairing and I could barely see where the feathers were damaged. I told him that I didn't think that he had to repair that one as I could barely find the damage. Uncle just looked at me for a while, and then he asked me what it was that the wand I held in my hand was. I said that it was a Brush Dance wand. Uncle waited for a while and then asked me what it was for and I told him it was for wearing in your head ring when you danced the Brush Dance. And that since one danced at night no one could see that it was very slightly damaged. He looked at me some more and finally he said, "But I know."

We sat in the sun and I helped him fix the wands. After a while he said that it was about time that I should begin to study to be a man. He would start asking me the questions that a man must be able to answer so that I could understand the law

I asked Uncle what was so hard to understand about the law. It seemed very simple to me because there was but one law and that was merely "Be true to thyself." Uncle asked me, "If you understand the law, why do you not understand why I am fixing my wands?" This I could not answer.

So he said to me, "Let us start over again. What is it that you are holding in your hand?" I answered, "A wand." Uncle made no answer. He quietly kept on repairing his feathers. After he had finished he put them away and went to work chopping wood for his fire. When he had finished his wood he got out his dip net and mended it and started down to the beach to see if he could catch some fish for breakfast. He still spoke not a word to me. I asked him if I could go fishing with him. He merely looked at me and said nothing. I could not understand why he wouldn't speak to me. Finally I asked him what was the matter. Had I offended him? He smiled and said no, that it was he who had not wished to offend me by interrupting my thoughts before I had finished answering the question.

I said, "But I answered the question. I told you what it was." He just looked at me some more and said nothing.

So I thought and thought and thought. Finally I told him, "It is a head wand for the last night of the brush dance." He looked at me and slightly smiled and said "Ehh," by which I knew that he meant "Yes, that's a little better, it will do as a start; now let's go after the answer." So I said, " It is to show how rich you are because it is the best and most expensive of all of the wands on the river." Whereupon Uncle looked upon me with disgust and said, "I thought that you wished to be a man. Why don't you start to think like one?" After having so expressed himself he left and went fishing. Not one more word was addressed to me that day.

The next morning Uncle was again sitting in the sun in front of his house. This time he was making some bone arrows points. He had been soaking the bone for several weeks in the creek and it was nice and soft and just right for cutting into shape. I sat beside him to watch how he carved the bone and to see how he cut with the grain so as to cut more easily. Finally he looked at me and said "Well?"

This was very bad for me. For Uncle only spoke this way when he was very, very angry. I had seen big, grownup people cast their eyes aside and blush when he so addressed them in council meeting. I had even seen important men leave the council and start out on long pilgrimages to the high places when so addressed.

I was only a small boy, and so I just cried and ran and cuddled up to my dog and told my dog how hard it was for a little boy to have such a great man for an uncle. And my dog understood and licked my face all over, and especially my ears.

Presently Uncle came to me and inquired if my ears were now clean enough to listen with, and did I still wish to be a man?

I said, Oh yes, I did.

Uncle said that since I was such a little boy he would help me a little more. So I should tell him again what it was that the Brush Dance wand was. This time I told him that it was the wand which one wore in his head ring on the last night of the Brush Dance for the final curing of a sickness in the person for whom the dance was being held.

Uncle smiled and said that that was a little better, but what was the Brush Dance really all about anyway? I said that it was to drive out the evil spirits which were making the person sick. Uncle looked at me and shook his head. He said, "You sound like a superstitious old woman. I shall be kind to you this time and tell you all about it."

So he spoke: "When a person is sick with a sickness that people cannot see, it is then that for that person we hold a brush dance. In the brush dance we sing funny songs and make jokes to let that person know that there is fun in the world. While everyone dances around the sick person, the doctor talks to the patient about what it is that troubles him. When that person sees that he is surrounded by friends who are singing happy songs to make him feel better, then he feels that people care for him. He feels safe and tells the doctor what it is that bothers him, and the doctor tells the patient what he can do about his troubles.

"On the last night of the dance everyone brings out their very best costumes. These costumes represent hundreds of hours of very careful work. They are made of the rarest and most difficult to obtain materials. They have been kept in absolutely perfect condition. Never does a costume ever show any wear or that it has been used before. Everything is perfect. These costumes are the most beautiful things we have. Thus when one dances before the sick person in costume, it means that the dancer has cared enough for the patient to go to all that trouble in the hope that he can help the patient.

"Now, how could I respect myself if I only went halfway, or three-quarters of the way to help someone? If I'm not going to help all of the way it is better that I don't go to that dance at all. So when I make a Brush Dance the patient knows that I am all of the way for him. Then he feels reassured and will quite likely get well.

"This is what the Brush Dance wands represent. This is the way to be true to yourself. Now let us see if you can think like a man the next time we have a question."

Then it was that I saw that the law was not quite as simple as it appeared. I realized that to be a man meant to be proud to yourself in everything; you could never be less than all of yourself without breaking the law.

When I finally understood what a person who entered a Brush Dance was doing, I then wanted to know just what the dance meant. Why was it danced the way it was danced? I asked why the dancers did not all dance up and down in unison.

This was what Uncle said: "The dancers do not all go up and down together because the world is like a canoe. If everyone leans to one side of the boat together, and to the other side together, they rock the boat and pretty soon it turns over."

I asked what the solo dancers were doing when they jumped in the middle and acted so strangely. He said, "Don't you remember the story of how, when the world was reborn, Creation appointed the giant woodpecker to go around the world and report to him how things were going? So in this dance men who have a pure spirit jump in the middle and jerk their heads back and forth like a woodpecker and spread their arms and fly around and sing the woodpecker song and everyone wears woodpecker scalps and heads. This is to remind the great woodpecker spirit that there is someone who is sick and he should go and report it to Creation so that Creation will lend his strength to the doctor so that the sick person can get well."

Hunting Rabbits

The air was clean and bright and smelled like a new washed rock and the killdeer were kreeling over the fields. It was one of those days that can only happen in October.

We had taken the shallow canoe and gone gathering tule-potatoes in the shallow sloughs in the flood plane on the south side of the river.[2] We waded alongside the canoe and dug the potatoes out of the bottom mud with our toes. The canoe was full of potatoes and the longish shadows of late afternoon were forming and it would soon be time for going home.

We were standing on the bank drying off our legs in the late sun when Hipur said that he thought he saw some cottontail rabbits near a clump of tall grass and maybe we should go and catch them. I wondered how we should catch them when we had no bows or arrows or anything else. There weren't even any rocks to throw. Hipur laughed and said that for a great hunter like himself it was easy. All that you had to do was to get to one side of the sun and slowly creep up on the rabbit. When you were about fifteen feet away from it, you swiftly ran towards it. Then, hitting the ground hard with your feet and spreading your arms, you jumped high in the air so that the sun would cast your shadow on the rabbit, and you screamed like a hawk. The rabbit would think that you were a hawk and would freeze so that when you landed you caught it before it moved.

So that is what we did, and Hi-pur got his rabbit nearly every time but it took me a long time to learn how, mostly because I couldn't run without making any noise. We hunted rabbits until it was too dark to see them any more. I don't remember how many we got, but it was nearly half of a small sack full. Then we got in the canoe and paddled across the river to home.

It was long after dark before we got our boat to the landing and we were not very happy because for a long time we had seen that there was a fire at the landing place. This meant that there was someone there waiting for us, or maybe even getting out a boat to come and look for us. So we beat the sides of our canoe as we paddled and sang a song so that whoever was at the landing would know that it was us and that we were all right. Our songs were "Tule potatoes, I love you" and "Crazy about rabbits, rabbits, rabbits."

By the time we got to the landing everybody was laughing at our silly songs and they were glad to see all the food, and Grandmother said she had been wanting some rabbit skins for a blanket. So it ended all right but we would always remember to make a fire next time and carry some glowing sticks in the boat so the people would know we were all right and where we were.

(When I was finally able to always shoot small game in the head and not spoil any meat, my uncle gave me his father's first bow. I was very proud and never again threw rocks at anything.)

Harry (left) with children of the Spott houshold, 1917

When I Grow Up

The wind was soft on our skins as we lay half hidden in the marsh grass and watched the river otters playing on the clay slide in our swimming hole. We had gathered many thimbleberry leaf baskets of salmon berries and were eating them while the sun dried us off.[3] It was one of those soft, warm, quiet days when the Mayflies dance and you can hear the earth hum.

I called my friend "Hi-pur" because he always played outways from the earth center at Kenek[4]. Whenever I went to find him at his home his grandmother pointed to Oregos, the great rock that guards the mouth of the river, and said *hipur*, which meant that he was down on the ocean beach learning about the ocean things. He usually called me *herkwer*, rabbits, like Roberts.

This day we had taken the canoe up the river into one of the sloughs that was in the spruce swamp to go swimming and to get salmon berries. We were all full of nice swim and fresh salmon berries and life was very good, and we talked of how we would like to be when we grew up.

Hi-pur said he would be a great hunter like his younger uncle and he would know all about how to be hunting all kinds of animals and fishes, and he would always keep a great big smokehouse full of smoked fish and deer and elk and especially smoked sturgeon, which is the best of all. But he didn't know if he could be a great hunter and a Man because there were no longer any sweathouses to make the early morning prayer fire.

I was going to study to know the law and I would go far back into the mountains to make my medicine to be a *man* like our elder uncle, and I would marry Hi-pur's sister and we would all live together in our family house.

So we lay in the sun and watched the otters play and spun our dreams of how it might be when I could walk with the spirits and find the deer and fish for him to catch so that we would have plenty of food. We thought of how it was that we should know if we could speak with the spirits and see the meaning of things, and if we were strong enough to face Creation and accept the law. We should have to put ourselves to the test all of the time.

The first test we could think of was to feel like a redwood tree and to see if our canoe would listen to us. So we spent the afternoon trying to think like a tree. Then we took turns with the canoe to see who it would behave best for. Hi-pur ran the canoe every which way like a log in the ocean. He finally got caught in a snag and we had to swim to get the canoe free. He said that he could talk to the ocean and he should stay off of the river where he couldn't make his canoe listen to him.

* * *

I pounded on the side of the canoe with my paddle handle until I could make a canoe-tree song. The canoe danced over the water and between the snags and my feet grew into the foot-rests and Hi-pur said he could not tell us apart as the canoe looked like me and I looked like part of the canoe, and it must be that I was able to talk to the spirit that was in the canoe, and maybe it was because I came from the beforetime people. We both thought that this might be because the redwood tree was a man in the beforetime. This is how it happened:

In the early days when it was that the Wo-gay lived here there was a very fine, big, strong man who lived right. When all of the world was to be cleaned by the flood this man was so fine and good that Creation took pity on him and said what would be best would be for the man to say what he would like to be after the flood. So the Wo-gay said that he would like to be a big, fine redwood tree for the new human beings to make houses and canoes of. So that is how it is that a canoe has a heart and a main artery and a face and a nose and a place for a necklace and why it wears a hat and a necklace.[5] And you can sing and talk to that spirit and the canoe will sing and talk with you, and you skim and dance over the river like so lovely.

Harry and Alice Spott upriver on the Klamath, ca. 1917

Salmon

The spring rains had come and everyone had gathered down on the bar to watch for the first run of salmon.[6] At the mouth of the river the people were crowding both banks watching for the fish to come. The young men, who were showing how brave they were, were standing far out on the sand spit where the ocean waves nearly broke over them. For it was a great thing to be the first one to see the salmon come, and it would bring one good luck in his fishing. That one would be called "the-one-who-saw-the-first-salmon" all the rest of that season and this was a very great thing to be called.

We children, Hi-pur and myself especially, were in high spirits, for Grandmother and Uncle had given us the scented herbs from the high mountains to cast into the river for the salmon to smell so that they would know how to find their way into the river.[7]

Ta-alth and the younger children were standing in a line to the ocean side of Up-River Uncle to cry out the coming of the first fish so that he could talk to it and greet it and thank it for bringing the winter food supply and to remind it to rub off a few scales at each of the fishing places as it went up the river so that the rest of the salmon would know where to stop to be caught so that everyone would have his winter fish supply. This was a great honor for the young ones to share.

*   *   *

The greatest fun would be when the second fish came up. Then the children would jump and cry out "Fish! Fish!" and tall, handsome Up-River Uncle would stand forth into the river with his great long fishing spear held ready, and all of the people would be watching him and giving him their power.

When finally the fish came and Up-River Uncle cast the spear deep into the rushing water, everyone held their breath to see how it was--whether he speared the fish or not. But we children jumped with joy and assurance, for was not this our uncle the greatest of all men with his spear? Who had ever seen him miss his cast? And besides, had not we children been the ones who guided the fish to his casting place? Surely we had called the fish most properly. And our herbs were of the finest this year, for had not some of them come from the sacred rocks of the High Country where great men went to make their medicine? But it did seem so long since his spear had thrust itself deep into the water, and the line had floated slack in the eddy around Uncle's legs.

Then we saw the line snap out straight and Uncle grasped it and waded to shore as he pulled in the line. Finally out came the handle of the spear and Uncle grasped it and drew forth from the river the great salmon. It was the largest, most beautiful salmon I had ever seen and it flashed with iridescent colors as it splashed in the shallow water as Uncle drew it onto the beach and held it up for all the people to see. It was then that a great shout of "ayi-ee" went up as the people greeted the fish. And all of the people standing on the trails and hillsides shouted out, making so great a cry that it sounded as though the sky were falling. The spring salmon run started and everyone was spearing fish or catching them in long handled dip nets, and soon the beaches were covered with salmon.

It was then that the fires were built up and all of the children went to gather green willow sticks to put the salmon to cook before the fires.[8] The old women made basins in the sand by the riverbank to leach acorn meal for soup and mush and the young women brought baskets of dried berries and manzanita berry meal, and some brought bundles of bay leaves to put on the fire to flavor the fish, and huge baskets of water were heated for tea and the big feast of the first salmon began.

Then we all sat around the fires while the old women turned the fish and everyone rejoiced because Up-River Uncle had speared the fish on the first cast and that meant that fishing would be easy. And the fish was the largest ever seen for the first run and that meant that the fish would be large and fat and everyone would have all of the food they wanted and there would be plenty left over for inviting friends and visitors to share. There would be big gambling games and big dances and even a big smoke when great men from many days' travel would come to share our good fortune and to keep up their friendship.

*   *   *

And then when the fish and mush and tea were all cooked we all sat around the fires and ate and ate and ate and ate and ate. And the old men told tales of how much better it was in the old days, and the women laughed at them, and everyone listened to the old stories of how the fish were made to live in the water so that everyone, even those who could no longer walk, could catch them for food. And how Creation made the law that the heads should all go to the old people because they needed soft rich meat to keep them well.

The old men and the old women sat full fed and warmed themselves around the fires and told us children the fairy stories of our people--how coyote got his tail, how men got fire, how the bluejay got his devil and on and on and on. And the young people disappeared and far down the beach you could see a little fire where a young man and a young girl sat and listened to the song of youth together.

We fell asleep, and our parents carried us children home and put us to bed.

Harry's Commentary:

There was a stone bowl for catching the grease from the First Salmon when it was cooking, a special stone bowl, always treated with the greatest care, which collected the dripping oil from the tail of the ritually cooking first fish. We felt that Creation made the bowl. Isn't it sufficient that Creation made it? The bowl was made, and who is to question why. Did you make it? Your father? Your ancestor? Name it that man who made that bowl. Creation made it.

When I say that Creation made the bowl, I do not tell you what tool Creation used. Perhaps a dog chewed it out; perhaps it was a stone in a stream that water formed; perhaps a man had a dream and so fashioned it. What difference does it make how it was formed? Does it matter whether a man crushed garnet for an abrasive, or used ordinary river sand? Or whether a dog hollowed it out, scratching with sand-covered feet?

The thing that does matter is that some agency of Creation did form the bowl, and that it is the bowl for catching the ceremonial oil.

Octopus

It had been stormy and all of us children were gathering limpets for chowder. The storm had washed away all of the sign and we couldn't find where the cockles were nested under the eel grass beds. The ocean was still too rough for us to venture out to where the good mussels grew because of the danger of a twelfth wave catching us, so we were working on the high rocks well away from the ocean surge. That is why we were gathering limpets.

Suddenly Hi-pur gave a great shout for all of us to "Come see! Come see!" And there in a shallow tide pool was a huge octopus. We had never seen such a monster as this although we had always looked for one. The old people said that they were often washed ashore in heavy storms. Most of the octopuses were small, only as big as a cantaloupe, but this one was nearly as big as a washtub.

We didn't know what to do with it because we didn't know how strong it would be. So all of us stood around the tide pool with long sticks to keep it in the pool, and Hi-pur ran home to get Uncle to come and show us what to do.

Uncle came running down to the beach with a paddle from his canoe. He said that he had never seen an octopus quite this large before in a tide pool. Our uncle carefully waded into the pool with his paddle and put the broad blade of the paddle right up close to the octopus. Then gently, very gently, he took the octopus' arms one by one and wrapped them around the blade and handle of the paddle. This took a long time because for each two arms our uncle wrapped around the paddle the octopus let go with one arm. Finally all of the arms were wrapped around and the octopus was lifted out of the water. Uncle put the paddle with the octopus on it over his shoulder and we all went up the trail to home to show Grandmother what we had caught.

Grandmother was waiting outside of her house and when she saw what we had she cried out, for she was happy to see such fine food for the house. She told us to get a big tub of water on the fire and she soon had it boiling and our uncle put the octopus into the boiling water, paddle and all. Then he pulled the octopus out to clean it and prepare it for cooking.

We stretched its arms out and it was nearly eighteen feet across and everyone came to see how large it was and everyone began to call Hi-pur "the giant octopus finder," and he was very proud and Grandmother gave him the best part to eat--the body wall which is pounded and cooked like abalone, only it tastes even better than sturgeon. The next day we all had octopus chowder and it was the most wonderful chowder I have ever tasted. And all of us children felt very proud because we had done such a wonderful fishing and we had gotten all of the food for the family and everyone said how good it was to have such great fishermen in the family.

This made us feel fine and useful and important, and we were treated with honor and respect just like adults were.

Harry's Commentary:

In an Indian community or family, each individual was given credit for what he did. A person earned respect by his accomplishments. When one succeeded in achieving adult proficiency in any field of endeavor, one was considered and treated as an adult in that field. The chronological age of a person had nothing to do with one's standing--you were judged only by what you did.

For example, our grandfather had hunted and killed important game with his toy bow when he was a child. This demonstrated his maturity as a hunter and a small sinew-backed hunting bow was made for him, and he assumed his position as a man in hunting parties.

He had all of the rights, privileges and responsibilities of an adult hunter--this when he was about eight years old. Of course, he was not expected to kill deer or elk because his bow was only about one fifth the size of a man's bow and had a pull of about thirty five pounds. A man's bow for hunting had a pull of from eighty to a hundred and twenty pounds. For small game he had a light bow with a pull of forty to fifty pounds.

When I was finally able to always shoot small game in the head and not spoil any meat, my uncle gave me his father's first bow. I was very proud and never again threw rocks at anything.

Where there are no people There is no sin

I believe that I got this from George Flounder, early on. I didn't understand it too well then, just took it at a superficial level: when no one's there, no one messes up. But, of course, it means more. When there is no awareness, there's no wrong. For example, we felt that young children were without sin because they are not yet aware as people, not fully conscious.

The sky
is where the earth thins out
Infinity
is where
the sky thins out

It was around 1931-32, long after I'd made my first medicine, after my first wife died and I'd remarried, but before I had children. I was sitting in the grass on the point at the mouth of the river. Uncle and I had been talking about these things for a few days and I made this song. It's just a man's philosophy--daydream talk; what he does when he just goes and sits in the grass.

It's an obvious statement. I have lived this way all of my thinking life, since I was ten or something. I can't see a breath of air as any more than a drink of water. As I need air and water, so I need infinity.

And in a sense infinity is like Spirit, because it never ends.

The rock Oregos at the mouth of the Klamath River, ca. 1917

Jump Dance Song

One time Hi-pur and his brother and sisters and I were playing rock tag on the ocean beach. This tag was to run through the sand and stand on a rock to be safe or, where the beach was mostly rocks, to run over the rocks to a spot of sand.

After we got tired of playing tag we sat on the rocks just above the waves and ate seaweed and Hi-pur talked to the sea lions and they swam up to talk to us. After a while the girls got tired of this and gathered some wood and went home. We boys stayed and had a barking contest with the sea lions.

After a while there were a few candle fish washed up on the beach and we caught them. There were only a few so we went up to the house for some fire and told Grandmother for them not to worry; we would eat on the beach. We made our fire and watched the sunset and ate candlefish and seaweed and acorn bread and sweet grass. We thought to keep the fire burning so the people would know where we were and not worry about us, and we could run up and down the beach kicking the wet sand to see the sparks the phosphorous made. When we got tired we went back to our fire and cooked some more candlefish and sat by the fire listening to what then ocean was saying. But the ocean got very quiet and didn't talk to us. Finally I got a feeling that I should go to one side away from the fire and sit and look at Oregos.[9] So I told Hi-pur what I was going to do and for him to keep the fire going.

I went to where I felt it was to be the place to stop and I sat there very quietly wondering why I should feel that I should do this. After a while I heard a noise among the rocks at the base of Oregos, and finally I heard it clear that some people sang the Jump Dance song there. I walked up closer to the rocks, but then the singing stopped. Then I went back to where I had been, and they sang again, clear and loud. I made a sign for my friend to come over, but when he got to me they stopped their song again.

We didn't know what it meant, so we went home very fast. We were not frightened--we were simply very cautious--and it seemed appropriate that we leave at once as it was getting late and the people might worry about us.

It took us several days to get up courage enough to see Elder Uncle about what I had heard. Uncle was a very great man; he was more than a man; he was one who could "walk in beauty" and speak with the spirits. This thing I had heard was not to be taken lightly-- it could be very dangerous or very good for me, I didn't know. Neither of us had ever been told of such a thing happening.

We decided that since I was the one who had heard the song, I should go to Uncle alone, since whatever it was was obviously for me alone, as it stopped when Hi-pur came near. I asked Uncle if anyone ever heard singing at night among those rocks and he said yes. It was the Little People who were making a jump dance because the people had been talking about having a jump dance at Rekwoi but hadn't gotten around to making that dance. And the Little Pople who owned the jump dance got tired of waiting and were putting on their own dance. It comes about in this way:

In the days before the flood when the people were bad, some of the people were good. These people made themselves very little (about twelve to eighteen inches high) and rode out the flood on bundles of sticks and bulrushes. Creation saw these people do this and asked them why they were trying to stay. The Little People said that it was so they could teach the new people how to make the world-renewing prayer and songs of the jumping dance. So Creation rained on them and washed all of their color out so they could not be seen. That is how we can't see them but only hear then. When there is a jump dance they always come and guard their songs and if there is an impure dancer they make him very sick so he can't dance. If the people don't make the world-renewing prayer then the Little People make the dance themselves, and if some person hears their songs then it is a good dance and the world is renewed in peace. But if no one hears it, their song, then it is bad times are for the world. The jump dance is for prayers that then people should keep the Law and have good thoughts and be pure.

I asked Uncle what it meant that I heard this singing. Then he told me that it was that I could hear the spirits and it would be good for me to make my medicine in the high mountains. He said that when a boy heard this, this is what it meant for him to do. When a grown person hears the songs it just means that they are good and pure, and that they should make a prayer and cast tobacco on their fire. The Little People will know and watch over them and they will be lucky.

So that is how I knew that I was to make my medicine in the high places and to become a Man and to learn the Law.

Harry's Commentary:

About these world-renewing dances: When a dance was put up everyone was happy and excited over going to the dance, for they would see old friends and sing old songs and sing new songs and meet new friends. The young men combed their hair until it shined bright as polished ebony and they wrapped their braids in their best sea otter bands. The young women gathered Sweet Herb and packed it in their hair so that their lovers would smell the perfume as they whispered, one to the other, during the breaks in the dances.

This was the time when we expressed our appreciation to the Spirit of Creation for having made the universe, when the old men sang the songs in the high language that speaks only in emotions, not in words. This was when we showed our best things, feathers, dentalia, medicine baskets or great obsidian blades and the sacred deerskins, the deep blue ones and the pure white ones. These things were held forth in the dance as we thanked Creation for all of everything and showed that we were proud, and not selfish in the face of Creation.

Love is the perfume of beauty

Mary Ann Spott gave me this when I was fifteen or sixteen, in reference to my first wife.

A newly married couple is in love. It's such a strange thing that they want to know what it is. So they ask Grandma--what could be more natural?

Love is like the cream on milk. It doesn't come right up; it has to sit overnight.

Requa canning factory fishermen at the mouth of the Klamath,
ca. 1917

Ocean Girl

Ta-alth and I were nestled into a pocket of ferns and salal at the base of the land-slip where it comes to the beach. we were protected from the sea wind and the warm afternoon sun had broken through the fog and warmed us. We were eating salal berries with a few late strawberries and blackberries while our lily bulbs were roasting in the hot sand under our beach fire.

We often came to the land-slip because the lily bulbs were easy to dig in the loose earth there. Next to the sweet bay nuts, we liked the roasted bulbs of the brodiaea best. We were waiting for the tide to go out so we could get the large goose-necked barnacles that grew on the offshore rocks there. Grandmother had been feeling lonesy for the old times and was hungry for barnacles to eat, like when she was young and walked the trails behind her husband.[10] He had been a great hunter and Grandmother told us of how beautiful it was to look upon his broad shoulders and strong back with his long braided hair tied with sea otter fur, swinging nearly to his hips as he walked before her. He was such a man as one could follow so safely that one could pick the skin and sand from the barnacles and eat them like nuts while following him.

So we had come here today to get barnacles for her that she might make her memory more beautiful with the smell and taste and feel of them.

Ta-alth was humming a soft sweet song to herself. It was a song I had never heard before. It sounded like pure white sea foam floating before a south wind on a gentle ocean. I asked her what her song was for, and she told me it was for the beautiful ocean maid not to come and take me from her.

In the olden times before the flood and before the bad times, when all of the people and animals and trees and rocks talked the old language and could speak together, this is the way it was:

Pa-a was the eldest son of the headman of Saal. He was tall and slim and so beautiful that all of the flowers turned their heads toward him when he passed. His step was so light that it did not shake the dew from the spider webs in the path as he stepped along it. One could only tell that he was passing by hearing the pure sweet song that his spirit was always singing.

This day he was to come to the ocean to make his prayer for the setting sun and to see if the sun would give him a sign that he should speak with the spirits. If your spirit was pure and open and you walked in beauty then just as the sun disappeared you would see, for an instant, a beautiful clear blue green sparkling light where the sun had set. This was the most beautiful thing that you could know. Some thought that it was the pure light shining from the spirit of Creation.

Pa-a had come and made his prayer and seen his light, and he was standing at the edge of the surf. Before him in the surf there swam up a beautiful white fish, and it looked at him for a bit. Then slowly it turned into a white-skinned woman and she stood before Pa-a clothed in her beauty.[11]

She spoke to him and said, "You have for many times come here to make your prayer. Always I have seen you receive the sign of purity and beauty. You do not know what you prayed for, for many men have made this prayer but none have been as pure as you. So now you see what is was you have made this prayer for."

She then walked out of the water and took his hand and they went up the beach and made their place for staying and they joined their spirits and were man and wife.

In the morning they went to his father's house and Pa-a and his wife told the father what had happened and how he would have to go to the other land across the ocean to live, as his wife was a spirit person and their children would be spirit children and their beauty would be too bright for ordinary people to stand.

The father and mother of Pa-a were so happy and proud that they cried all day and washed their son and their daughter in their tears.

That evening as the sun set they all went to the beach and the wife of Pa-a turned back into a fish and carried him into the sunset. And when they went through all of the sky was filled with the beauty of the light of Creation.[12]

This is why it is that now sometimes a person who is pure in spirit can see this light, because it is Pa-a sending his greetings to his parents.

Ta-alth said that she was afraid that the daughter of Pa-a would take me from her before I should make my medicine and earn my tobacco baskets and then for what had she been working so hard to learn to make beautiful baskets if she couldn't make mine when I became a man?

And I pointed to the beach asters and said that these flowers were not as she was because they were not looking at me as she was, so she must be foolish to think I was so beautiful.

And I wondered why she told me that I was just stuck up and she got tears in her eyes and ran home and left me to get the grandmother's barnacles alone.

But when I got to the house with the barnacles the grandmother gave me some cookies made of pine nuts and brodaiea bulbs and sugar pine syrup that she said Ta-alth had just made for me, but Ta-alth was hiding in the brush and I could not find her to thank her. And the next day when I saw her she was mad at me because she said if I had really tried I could have found her, and that I was never to see her again.

So I felt sad because I did not like to walk the trails without her, and I asked Uncle what was the matter with her. He laughed at me and said I should go talk to grandmother, and it might be a good idea if I got one of those rings at the store that were set with a beautiful piece of abalone shell, and just maybe Ta-alth would wear it and go after clams with me on the next low tide. And that is what she did, but she wouldn't talk about the ocean maiden again.

And so I told Uncle that girls were very strange and I did not understand them. And he laughed at me again and said that men were always having the same kind of trouble with women. And that was the way of women.

It was then that I knew that though Uncle was among the wisest there were some things that even he didn't understand.

Spectators at a gambling game, Requa ca. 1917

Canoe

One time Waits-for-Fish decided that he needed a new boat. He went up into the redwood forest to hunt for a boat tree. That is, one that is about the right size and has tight wood so that it won't easily split or crack.

Waits-for-Fish found a very good tree and cut it down, cutting off the second log above the base to make his boat. A boat tree must not have any branches on the quarter that you will make the boat from, otherwise there would be knots in the hull.

So Waits-for-Fish found a boat tree and felled it and sawed it into a butt section and three boat sections eighteen feet long. The butt and top sections he sold to me and I sold them to a sawmill. Waits-for-Fish kept the two extra boat logs, for someone else might need to make a boat, too.

He rolled his logs down near the creek and covered them with leafy branches so that the wood wouldn't check. Then he took his wedges and split off the knotty side of the logs and sold these to me also. He took his first boat log and started to chip off the sapwood in order to make his canoe. But soon Waits-for-Fish found that he had made a very great mistake.

*　　*　　*

He had set up his log near a road where everyone who passed could see and talk to him. While he was busy chipping off the sapwood this was all very well, for the visitors most often lent a hand and chipped off the sapwood with him and he had much company, many songs and workers to lighten this rather tedious labor. But came the day when he started to shape this boat--his boat--and Waits-for-Fish found that those who had helped chip off the sapwood felt entitled to do a bit of chipping on the heartwood, too. This would have been a help except that each one had a different idea of how a canoe should be shaped. Presently Waits-for-Fish observed that the lines of the boat went one way and then they went another way, and he thought that the canoe might get confused and never know which way it was meant to go.

So Waits-for-Fish drew up a second boat log beside the first one and started to make a new canoe. Whenever anyone came by and wanted to help him work on his boat he gave them the tools and said that they should work on "everybody's canoe" and keep him company while he worked on *his* canoe. And this is what they did.

Finally both canoes were finished and both were put into the river. Waits-for-Fish's canoe was a joy to paddle for it skipped over the water in beauty and went just where you wanted it to go. But Everybody's Canoe didn't seem to know where you were wanting it to go. It seemed to go wherever you didn't want it to go, as though it couldn't make up its mind what was expected of it. Waits-for-Fish left this canoe tied up at the beach with a slipknot so that everyone would know that it was everyone's boat and could always be borrowed without asking permission. For many years we saw this boat tied up at any place where someone had left it. But no one could ever make it behave because it was too confused. So people only used it when they had to.

<u>Harry's Commentary:</u>

This story was given to me by Sregon George.

When it be that you fell a redwood for to make a canoe you gather sweathouse wood for ten days (more better twelve days).[13] Then you go into the redwood forest and sing it to the tree how it is that in the Wo-gay times it was a man who said he would be a redwood for making a canoe out of after the flood. You sing it out this song as you go through the forest and after a while you will hear a tree call out your name and say "here I am." You go over to that tree and you clear away all of the brush from around it and you pat its bark and tell it how smooth and straight and beautiful it is. You make a little fire and smoke a pipe for the tree and you put your pinches of tobacco dust on the coals so that he can have his pipe, too. You keep up getting sweathouse wood and sweat bath for twelve more days. Also, on his fire you put all kinds for fish and seaweed and mussels, clam, etc., so you get him that tree hungry for fishing.

*   *   *

Now that tree be so hungry to go fishing every day and he so happy to have someone to love him that he nearly falls down by himself. (This is seriously reported to have sometimes happened.) At any rate, the tree is cut down and made into a canoe.

**The heart of the tree
holds its history
Without heart the tree
cannot stand**

I'd asked Robert Spott why I had to learn so much about what went before me in the study: "Why do I have to learn all this about what happened in the old days when this isn't happening now?"

If you destroy history in a tree it has nothing to stand with. If you destroy heart you have nothing to stand with. The two are completely related. Stand is live. You can say,

**The heart of the tree
holds its history
Without history the tree
cannot live**

That's still correct. There are lots of ways to say it and still be right. In old-time Indian it would be,

**Tree inside old tree.
No inside,
fall down.**

You can go on and on with this one, getting down through it, asking the next question. Ask the right question:

> ### Young roots feed the plant
> ### old roots support it

But,

> ### One is no longer what one was
> ### One is what one is
> ### Circle back, get it:
> ### If not here before
> ### not here now

There is nothing new in Creation. You learn it, that, then you can see.

Tumult is the gas of frustration

George Flounder gave me this during the time when I was training hard, before I made *man*. I didn't see any point in running the mountain every morning and getting into a steam-heated sweat, because all that happened was that I got into a steam-heated sweat. I'd boiled the pot out. I was through, disgusted--at least that's what George said.

But this was only the beginning. I had to dig deeper until I understood what "tumult" is. So, if you want to develop this, you can go on to find out what the "gas of frustration" is, why it's a gas, and so on. Or you can leave it and go on to another subject. But even if you chase it to the end you'll still find two things to consider. There are always two sides to the coin, always.

You can't write a book about such things, the way that's usually tried, because you can only write about you. But, then, you might find someone as crazy as yourself and in the same way and read what he's written and that might help a little.

When you think about tumult you see that you can't tell someone who doesn't understand tumult what tumult is. When you get to this point you are thinking about teaching, and that's a hard point to get around. When you try to teach someone about something beyond their experience you have to go beyond sight; you have to go to insight. You have to push them and that's what's hard in teaching.

There is so much that the early anthropologists could never get from the old-timers: it was just too personal. I've never told these things to white men, either, because I worry that I won't be understood. That's what the old people used to say: "We just want to be understood." That's *all* they wanted, but when they realized that the anthropologists and psychologists couldn't understand them, they stopped speaking of personal things or developed things and only gave them what they could understand. That's the law: don't give people what they can't understand.

I hope people are ready to understand more now. I have to trust you.

The fawn lies quiet
in the grass
The lily
does not sing

I made this one evening after I'd been making small medicine. Mostly what you make small medicine for is to get accumulated--you get upset, you go off, settle down. You make medicine. The world is beautiful again. It's a personal thing, private and peaceful. It's nothing very big, but nothing very little either.

Creation

In the beginning there was just Spirit. Spirit is made of Spirit-stuff. It is not a solid substance or a gas, just Spirit-stuff, which is different from physical-stuff. It is a force, an energy, which creates and exists yet has no form or dimensions. It makes all things of itself yet is itself neither diminished nor consumed. It is timeless and limitless.

Each thing is given its own spirit while behind each spirit is the Spirit of Creation, or just Spirit. So there is only one Spirit and all things are as one. I call it "Spirit" or "Creation," but those are just words; it is everything.

To understand this force one has simply to accept it and to accept one's own position in it. It is impossible to tell somebody that if you are in complete acceptance of Creation you will not have even a concept of the feeling of fear, but this is true.

When the white man came the Indians tried to tell them about Creation and the white men called it, "The Great Spirit." However, this was conceived of as an overgrown personification of a man who lived somewhere in the sky, like Jehovah, and this was far from what was meant.

*   *   *

An ant is physically and mentally limited; it cannot conceive of the earth. Man is in the same position in the face of Creation. To personify Creation in the form of a man or a god is juvenile. A man is one who can stand alone and does not need a god to blame things on. But the facts of life are that very few people are strong enough in spirit to stand alone; they need crutches to support themselves. (I suspect that these are 'the the lame and the halt and the blind' that Jesus miraculously cured so that they could see and throw away their crutches.)

Of course, if there is no personification of God, there need be no devil, either.

Since the Yurok had no personified God they had no name for God. The European insisted on having a name so some Yuroks said "Wohpekumew," who put everything in order in the beginning, was God.[14] But others gave a word that meant "creation" [ki 'wes'onah] or "to exist," "to be" or "that is." Sometimes people used a word like nahkwok' [it does] meaning by it, "You see how it is like but there are no words to say it." The description of Creation was usually given by an expressive opening gesture of the hands. Still, I call it "Creation."

Creation is everything. The old-timers felt that an understanding of Creation could be achieved through the study of beauty.[15] The world was seen as beautiful and their prayer was, "May I walk in beauty." Today there is art but much art is ugly because there are no spaces, and spaces are where the spirits walk in the beauty of Creation.

Before, when a man made communion with Creation so that he could walk in beauty he stood forth on a mountain top and opened his hands and held his arms wide and looked full into the breaking dawn and let the Spirit of Creation flow into him. He didn't even wear moccasins or a necklace lest some portion of him should be shielded from the light of Creation. To these men it seemed very strange to see their grandchildren clasp their hands together to hide something and bow their heads and close their eyes to hide their spirit when they were hidden behind walls and call that prayer.

But these were real *men*. I don't mean big bruisers stomping around, but complete people. We say "man," but some of them have been women. These people became complete by studying very hard, training hard from their early life on.

**Sea foam is a bit of ocean
captured by the wind
Sea foam is a bit of wind
captured by the ocean**

This is my own. Robert was teaching me how to think. I was asked what sea foam was? Robert could ask the stupidest questions.

He was satisfied with my answer. If he hadn't been it wouldn't be here. In fact, he chuckled. He seldom chuckled.

Harry Roberts in the mid-1950s

Training I

I have tried in the stories to give a sense of the way a Yurok child grew up in my day. In some ways it was quite different from the growing up of a European-American child of the United States of today, but in some ways it was similar. Both societies send their children to school from about their sixth to their eighteenth years. The schools are about equal in the amount of study required. However, our grading system was somewhat different. If a modern American child comes within 60% of completing an examination he passes the grade and is promoted. If a Yurok came within 1% of hitting and killing a deer he flunked and went hungry. There is no meal that is slimmer than one composed of an almost-caught fish. So the old Yurok way of life led to a very strict philosophy that I think is well illustrated by a parable my uncle once told me:

"If you go swimming, go into the water all the way and get washed all over and feel good and clean all over. Then come out all of the way in the sun and get nice and dry and warm all over. Then you feel good all over.

"If you only go in swimming half way all you get is a wet bottom. If you come out of swimming half way all you've got is a wet bottom. A wet bottom all of the time is no way of living."

*   *   *

It was Uncle's unsolicited opinion that most white people have a wet bottom most of the time.

A Yurok child in the old days did not have to be anything but himself. He was born an ignorant baby. He could grow up to be a man, but there were all stages of maturity between childhood and manhood and one was not forced to achieve a level that one didn't wish to achieve. If a Yurok child studied hard and became a real person he was known as such and bore the title "man." All over North America, as far as I know, such titles simply mean, "an all-grown-up person, a *man*." The Europeans observed that these Indians were without fear and gave them the title of "brave." This sort of manhood was very difficult to achieve and the number of *men* in a tribe was never very large. Among the Yurok of the lower Klamath River, from the ocean to about fifteen miles up, there was an adult male population of about three hundred. Of this number there were usually from ten to fifteen *men*.

The old Yurok operated on a strictly monetary basis, and all values were reduced to a price in money. Real *men*, including women who were medical doctors, were able to make the most money.[16] It stood to reason, then, that when a young person wanted to study to be a *man* he had to make financial arrangements with his teachers. In ordinary childhood training the whole community chipped in: small boys and girls hanging around the family-house were taught by the old men and old women and these people were in turn supported by a percentage of the fish, game, and nuts that were gathered by the more able.

However, when a boy went to study in the sweathouse to become a *man* he had to pay all of the cost himself and it could be pretty expensive. A teacher who had very powerful medicine charged accordingly, like Stanford or Yale does. With the Yurok, though, there was one difference. If you didn't get educated--or if you didn't get cured by a doctor you'd hired--you got your money back.

In essence, there is really only one law: Be true to yourself. All that a Yurok teacher does is to point out to the student that he is either being true to himself or not.

When a person studies to be a man he is really studying to be himself. He looks at what he is, what he does, what he does not do. Then he measures what he *is* against that which is true. Slowly, he finds all of the false things and cleans himself of them. Of course this process is guided by many rules--what people now call taboos, I guess--but these rules simply reflect the pattern of things. The hunting animal makes his hunting trails and it is a foolish bird that makes a nest in the hunting trail of a cat. Maybe these rules reduce to a few simple ones:

All things have patterns, or paths.

*   *   *

Learn to see the paths of Creation. If you are a *man* you will walk in beauty.

There are paths of impure thoughts. Don't put your foot on or into these. If you are not a man you will walk in falsehood and selfishness.

Do not walk on a path that someone with impure thoughts has walked upon; it is contaminated.

Don't purchase something good with bad money. It is forever contaminated and the purity of beauty will be besmirched. The aura of bad thoughts lingers on.

You are what you practice. If you practice anger you are angry and full of hate. If you practice seeing beauty you will be beautiful.

Because man is limited, like an ant, he cannot make judgments upon the demonstrations of Creation, which his mind is too rudimentary to conceive of. He cannot question Creation. Creation is, and it is a *man's* prerogative only to observe and accept, not to judge. Children judge, but a *man* is beyond such childishness. So, if a *man* is confronted by strange perceptions, he doesn't make the judgment that they do not exist, but he accepts them as another phenomenon in Creation. He observes, studies, and sometimes masters them--like he would a rock or a fish or any physical object.

When a person studies to be a *man* he is only learning to look at things as they really are.

This is not easy for people to do because we always censor our own thoughts. What we do, or say, or think, is always subject to this censorship. Self-criticism alters the true sense of our thoughts and it is hard for a person to become aware of the judgments that he imposes on his own thinking. One may look at a familiar object in a strange situation and because the object 'should not' be there, thinks it is something else or even does not see it at all. All training for manhood is training to see, and mind is just another thing in Creation.

Often the censor is what someone else may think of you: "they." But the law is "Be true to yourself," and this means simply that one must face himself as he is and not as he might think someone else wishes him to be. A man never cares what "they" might think; he is only concerned about how true he is to himself.

But if a person is to be free, he must not only be free of other people's censorship but he must also be free of his own judgments against himself. People not only censor their thoughts before they voice them, but sometimes before they even become aware of them. To censor your speech is a sensible thing to do when you know what you're doing and why and when you don't do it because of what "they" might think. But when a man makes his medicine what he really accomplishes is the removal of the censor that censors his thoughts before he thinks them. This is the hardest part of training--really brutal.

Sometimes this censor just won't go and it may take many years of training before it does. But only then is a person master of himself and a *man*. Such *men* have remarkable clarity of thought.

> ***When the waves of time***
> ***wash the sands of time***
> ***there is that***
> ***which washes free***
> ***of time***

I can only guess who gave me this because I don't remember clearly. It sounds so much like Robert Spott that I'd like to say it's him, but it isn't. It's one of my teachers--I'd guess George Flounder, but that's only a guess.

I'd asked a question, before I made my medicine. It was not a 'passing question,' one you had to answer before you could study further. The question behind this one is one of those that you grow with. The way you answer such questions tells your teacher how far you are with your studies. I don't think so hard on these as I do, say, on a law question; I don't have to strain my milk on it; these are just stupid questions.

Another way to answer (or ask) this question goes like this:

> ***Windrows of sea moss***
> ***etch transient patterns***
> ***on the changing***
> ***sands of time***

A more direct, Indian-English translation of that is,

Dead seaweed designs on beach sand
Beach sand all time moving

You have to ask what is it? When? Where did it happen? Well, who cares? It happened. There is that part of what happens with the study through time that washes free of the limitations of time--and then it's a new ballgame.

Getting rid of the pish-posh is what the study is really about.

Harry netting shad in the early 1970s

Training II

Freedom does not come easily but only through hard training.
There were, in the old days, many ways to train. One of them was
running up a mountain in the morning to gather special firewood
for the sweathouse fire. When we do this we pray with a song, a
chant. One such prayer is like this:

> I will see me as I am
>
> I will be like I am
>
> I will find out what I am
>
> I will not hide what I am
>
> I am as pure as Creation
>
> I am strong as Creation
>
> I am part of Creation
>
> I am a *man*

One of these lines is chanted each morning, and then the list is
repeated four times.

Training for man is a matter of learning to ask the right questions
of oneself. This usually means that one simply states the true
problem. All excuses and rationalizations must be discarded, for
they are simply masks that one puts on in order to refuse to admit
or accept the facts of any given situation. The point is to be able

to think clearly about everything, every time. The Yurok word for 'bad' is better understood as "unsuccessful, the word for 'good' as "successful." If a person arrives at a conclusion by accident, by guessing, the conclusion is no good. He must go back to the beginning and start all over again--all the way back, because only things done step by step, in order, can be successful.

Here is another chant for running after sweathouse wood:

People are people

People are small

People are weak

People find excuses for their weakness

I am a people

I am weak

I am to be a *man*

I am to face the facts

I am not to make excuses

I am a *man*

I can face myself

This prayer is chanted once through each day. It is thought about. While making such prayers, you look at yourself as you are, good and bad, everything that you are. You look at it as it is.

This kind of training that I have been talking about produces individuals who are dependent on themselves alone, who have no need to take either physical or spiritual things from others.

People study and meditate and finally make a medicine run into the mountains. Even with many years of preparation not everyone succeeds in getting their power and becoming *men*. But when power comes it comes suddenly and when a *man* once gets his power there is nothing that can defeat him. He may be killed, but never defeated. These *men* have different specialties and no *man* puts himself in the position of an all-knower, a god. He only makes his medicine so that he can accept the facts with which Creation has presented him. You are what you are and you have a right and a duty to be only that. A *man* must act to the standard of his training and to do otherwise would be selfish.

In the end you and you alone are the judge of your worth. You may be able to pull the wool over other people's eyes, but you can't kid yourself. At the close of every day a *man* makes his prayer. It's a very simple prayer, but I doubt that many people can make it. He makes it honestly, knowing that he has not always been wise, that he has not always done the best thing. He may have fallen flat on his face in failure; he may even, in ignorance, have caused pain and damage to others. The prayer is offered with a humble heart. I say it like this, more or less:

Today I have done the best I could do
with what I had to do it with
today

In all innocence
the avalanche
consumes
the valley

Either Fanny Flounder or Mary Ann Spott gave me this when my world crashed. There's a corollary that is interesting because it shows how we kept to pairs in most songs:

Stars shine
So comes sunshine

There are two others that the same people gave me around that time:

> **When the shadow**
> **falls**
> **there is no sound**
> **When hearts break**
> **there is only   silence**

> **The leaf is fed**
> **with sunshine**
> **The spirit is fed**
> **with love**

Harry walking in the redwoods near Gualala, Calif., early 1970s

The Lonesome Trail

The trail was lonesome. I had gone some little ways up it before I realized what it was that was wrong. So I had to go back and start over the trail again.

So I started over again, and I sang that trail the song to tell the trail how it was not forgotten and I would come along and keep it company. I had been thinking selfish thoughts and that was why I hadn't thought for the trail, how it felt.

I kicked the rocks and sticks from the path and I broke off the branches and twigs that were growing across it, and the trail became bright and cheerful and showed me itself where it was all overgrown and one could not see the path, where it went.

And the birds came back to the trail and sat on the bushes and sang to it. The ground birds came back and scratched the leaves and twigs off of it and made it a bright shiny trail again, and the squirrels gathered the nuts that rolled down the trail into nice neat piles. So I was able to walk along a happy singing trail, and this is the way it should be.

I had never been on this trail before so I didn't quite know where it went. I only knew that it went up the creek and that up the creek it would be quiet country where no people had been to leave bad thoughts, and that I was troubled in my thinking and should go where I could talk with the spirit of creation and find myself again.

The trail had started out on the creek flat where the creek entered the river valley. Here there were wide gravel and sand bars covered with salmon berries and alders and vine maples.

Soon it entered the creek valley and the creek bars had on them great broad-leafed maples whose arching branches and trunks were covered with thick moss that hung down for many feet in soft green curtains. I walked between huge hummocks of giant sword ferns that reached nearly over my head. Occasional patches of soft golden green sunlight filtered through the canopy overhead and lighted the forest floor, which was covered with a deep carpet of lush green moss with patches of Delft blue grouse flowers and soft arching sprays of the pink star-like flowers of Indian lettuce.

As I went farther up the trail the creek canyon narrowed until the trail was mostly along the ledge of the creek itself and I often had to scramble across the face of rocky cliffs or wade up the creek bed. Here the dense forest came down right to the creek and the creek tumbled over the gnarled roots of the giant redwoods and firs.

The forest floor was deep with redwood and fir needles and there were no green things, for no sunlight ever penetrated the dense forest cover. There were pink glowing pine drops and pure white ghost plants growing in the forest mould. There was no animal life on the forest floor, for there was no food here for the animals to eat. There were no cobwebs or insects, there was no sound, nothing but the silent throb of the earth itself. High above I could occasionally hear the passage of a flock of birds. Here it is that the tree mice live in the tops of the fir trees where they spend their entire lives and never come down to the ground.

And it is here, walking through the massive stillness of the primeval forest, that one must look upon one's self as he is. Here is the ghost of humanity that only a strong man can look upon without fear. For here is one of the places where there is naught to stand between one and the truth of Creation. This is a land wherein the spirits speak. This is where one's spirit is washed pure of the contaminations of petty thoughts and desires.

Further and further the trail led onward, until finally the creek opened out into a little flat, with soft grassy meadows bordered with alders. There were flowers and birds and butterflies all through the meadows and the creek had deep quiet pools of clear blue water with lovely shining trout swimming about. Here I felt it was, that which I had taken the lonesome trail to find.

I made my camp by the stream and built my fire, bathed in the pool and sat by the fire and smoked my pipe, and felt all clean because of my passage through the deep forest and my bath in the clear pool.

*   *   *

I sat by my fire all night and smoked my pipe and cast my tobacco dust onto the fire and felt the soft breath of the sky over my body. And in the morning I went to the ridge-top and greeted the rising sun and gathered wood for my sweat bath and gathered herbs from the mountain top to incense the smoke of my fire. And I returned to my camp and made medicine and became peaceful again.

All day I lay in the beautiful meadow and thought of the beauty and purity of creation. That night I kept my fire and smoked my pipe and cast the tobacco dust on my fire and listened to hear the spirit of Creation speak within me. So, as the deep of the night came upon me, I began to sing. And I sang until all of the darkness of the world came about me and enfolded me and my body became lost and my spirit came forth clean and free. And then I could sing the song of the dawn of creation and I could know again the lost language of the spirits and sing their songs in the presence of Creation. My spirit walked forth into the spirit land and became pure and peaceful again.

In the morning my spirit returned to my body and I woke up. The morning was bright and clear and beautiful and I was hungry, for I had not eaten for three days. I knelt beside the bank of the stream and put my hand down under the edge of the bank and I hummed the song of the fish talk and the trout swam into my hand and this way I caught enough fish for my eating.

And then it was that I could go back to the places where there were people, for I had come back into Creation and was renewed.

And what it was of small selfish things that the world of people valued and strove and fought for I was no longer bothering about, it so it did not matter what it was that had disturbed me and sent me to make my prayer. How can one put importance in childish desires when one has walked in beauty in the face of Creation?

This is the way it is for a *man*.

Notes

The spelling used for Yurok language words, in italics below, was created by the Yurok Language Program, Department of Linguistics, University of California, Berkeley, and follows the Preliminary Yurok Dictionary, *2005.*

1. The *woogey* are mythical "First People" or "Beforetime People," as Harry sometimes called them. When the Indians came, the *woogey* turned into animals and trees and rocks, went to the spirit world to dance, or stayed on earth to accompany the human beings, "the ones who camp here." --TB

2. Tule potatoes (*Sagittaria latifolia*) grow in water from a few inches to three or four feet deep. You wade around and feel for the tubers with your feet and scuffle them loose. The tule potatoes rise to the surface and float and are scooped up in a small dip-net and dumped into the boat. Wherever these were available the Yuroks gathered and preserved them as food for babies and old people because their starch is so easily digestible. --HKR

3. The thimbleberry bush has wide, soft, pliant leaves. These were fashioned into small containers secured with twigs for collecting, in this case, salmon berries. --HKR

4. Hi-pur *(hipur)* is a directional term meaning "northward; toward the river mouth; down below." --TB

5. These are all traditional design features of the Yurok carved redwood canoe, still being made on the river today. --TB

6. This story is part experience, part vivid re-imagining based on what Harry was told, and part what he knew directly of the environment. The last full, traditional Yurok First Salmon Ceremony

at *wehlkwew*, across the mouth of the Klamath from modern Requa, was held, according to historical records, in 1850. After that the spring salmon run had been drastically curtailed by the "Forty-niners'" upstream placer mining for gold, although something like it, though diminished, lasted at least into the twentieth century.

The nickname Ta-alth that appears below means "ceremonial dancer" (*taahl*) and "Up-River Uncle" was probably based on a Spott or Frank family relative of Robert (Frank) Spott's --in any case, a different uncle from the Uncle, Robert Spott, who appears in so many of Harry's other stories. --TB

7. In Harry's stories, "Grandfather" refers to Captain Spott, Robert Spott's adoptive father, and Grandmother refers to his wife, Mary Ann. --TB

8. You always got the cooking sticks *after* you caught the first salmon. To get them beforehand would be offensive: it would be an insult to the salmon to cook him before you catch him. --HKR

9. Oregos (*o regos*, Tucker's Rock) is a very large rock, now partially fallen, on the north side of the mouth of the Klamath River, one of two sisters stationed on either side of the river's mouth to guard it.

"Rekwoi" (*o rek'w*, modern Requa) stands on a hillside just upriver from Oregos and was traditionally one of the villages where the Yurok Jump Dance was put up. --TB

10. "Lonesy" is Indian English. It's a feeling--all alone and lonely. Sometimes you feel it in the high mountain valleys when you hear the trees weeping because the people are gone now and no longer come to see the beauty of that place. --HKR

11. The *woogey*, spirit beings, are said to be all white. Euro-Americans were called '*woogey* when they first appeared in the

19th Century in part because of their skin color, in part because they were from away. --TB

12. When the Yurok speak of going "through" that is to say 'through the crack between the worlds.' For them, the sky is a great bowl that comes down to meet the sea in the west, between the Earth and the Across-the-Ocean-Lands where many of the Wo-gay now live. The sky-rim rises and falls, making the ocean waves, striking the sea harder every twelve (or ten) times, causing an exceptionally large wave periodically. In winter the sky-rim strikes harder than in summer, making rough winter waves. --HKR

13. The grammar reflects what Harry heard as "Indian English." Since his stories are primarily based on experience with élite Yuroks (traditional Yurok society was stratified in complex ways), his language--as in this story told by Sregon George--often reflects the "high" register of Yurok spoken by the élite. It is a way of speaking both very precisely and also poetically, using a specialized vocabulary and piling up particles to achieve these ends. --TB

14. In Yurok mythology, Wohpekumew is one of the two (quite fallible) great trickster-creators of the world. The other is Pulekukwerek. Neither made the earth: they only put it into its now familiar order and rhythm. --TB

15. Harry rendered the Yurok *mrwrsrgerh* as "beauty." In Yurok it is a verb, 'to be beautiful' in the sense of being pure, unpolluted, able to make medicine and to take part in rituals. --TB

16. Harry refers to traditional "sucking doctors" here, *kegey*, most often female "shamans" who cured physical illness. Their training was notably long and arduous and they were sociological males, *pegrk*, the word Harry translates as "man." --TB